by Rebecca Phillips-Bartlett

Minneapolis, Minnesota

Credits
All images are courtesy of Shutterstock.com, unless otherwise specified. With thanks to Getty Images, Thinkstock Photo, and iStockphoto. Recurring – orangemoon, Gilmanshin, Tohuwabohu1976. Cover – Ian 2010, Gilmanshin. 4–5 – Singkham, na-dia_if, Subbotina Anna, Flower_Garden, Anna-Nas. 6–7 – Filipe B. Varela, malshkoff. 8–9 – dookfish, Pelevina Ksinia. 10–11 – Glass and Nature, Mr. Background, Pablesku. 12–13 – sergios, Viktor Loki, Hridoy Khan123. 14–15 – Nataly Studio, Amarita, domnitsky, Wut_Moppie, Tiger Images. 16–17 – Peeravit, Andruzzz, Ellen Bronstayn. 18–19 – Prostock-studio, chomplearn. 20–21 – Petr Levicek, Bill Florence, Maria Kaminska. 22–23 – Have a nice day Photo, Valeriya_Chistyakova.

Bearport Publishing Company Product Development Team
President: Jen Jenson; Director of Product Development: Spencer Brinker; Managing Editor: Allison Juda; Associate Editor: Naomi Reich; Associate Editor: Tiana Tran; Art Director: Colin O'Dea; Designer: Kim Jones; Designer: Kayla Eggert; Product Development Assistant: Owen Hamlin

Library of Congress Cataloging-in-Publication Data is available at www.loc.gov or upon request from the publisher.

ISBN: 979-8-88916-951-2 (hardcover)
ISBN: 979-8-88916-955-0 (paperback)
ISBN: 979-8-89232-128-0 (ebook)

For more information, write to Bearport Publishing, 5357 Penn Avenue South, Minneapolis, MN 55419.

CONTENTS

PLENTY OF PLANTS

Our world is full of many amazing plants. They come in different colors, shapes, and sizes.

Let's explore this *plant-iful* world all around us!

PLANTS CAN GROW IN THE GROUND, IN WATER, OR ON OTHER THINGS.

FABULOUS FLOWERS

Many plants grow flowers. These plant parts **blossom** and make seeds.

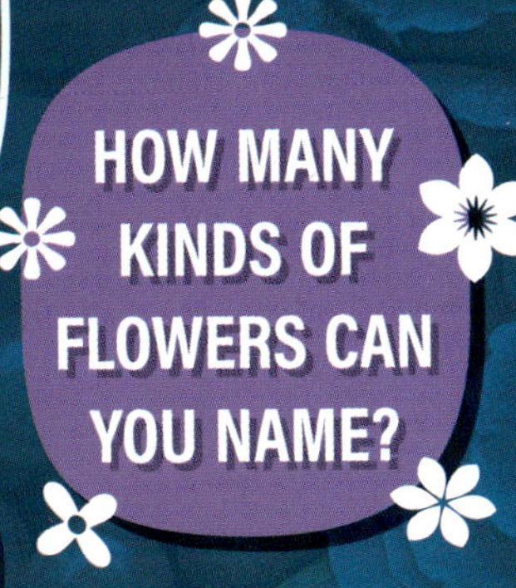

PLANT PARTS

Not every plant grows flowers. However, there are some things that almost all plants have.

ROOTS

Most plants have roots underground. These thin parts collect water and **nutrients** that help plants grow.

ROOTS ALSO HELP PLANTS STAY IN PLACE.

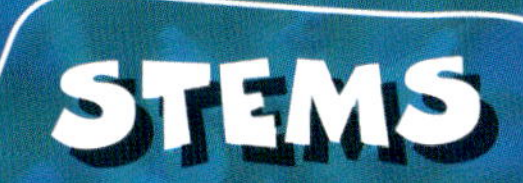

STEMS

Most plants have stems that help hold them up. The water and nutrients from the roots travel through the stem to get to the leaves.

FLOWERS USUALLY GROW AT THE END OF A STEM.

FLOWER FEATURES

Flowers are made up of parts that help some plants **reproduce**.

PETALS

Petals are often very colorful. Some smell good. The petals **attract** animals, such as **insects**, to the flower.

STAMENS AND POLLEN

Stamens are parts of flowers that make a powder called pollen. They look similar to stems with headlike parts at the top.

STIGMA AND CARPEL

The stigma collects pollen. From there, the powdery pollen goes into the carpel, where the flower makes seeds.

Stamen

Stigma

Pollen at the top of the stamen

Carpel

POLLINATION

Pollination is when pollen goes to a flower's stigma, allowing it to make seeds. Some flowers can use their own pollen or pollen from another flower on the same plant. This is called self-pollination.

SUNFLOWERS CAN SELF-POLLINATE.

Other flowers can't use their own pollen. They need pollen from the flowers of different plants. This is called cross-pollination. Flowers get this pollen when small animals travel from one flower to the next.

ANIMALS THAT HELP MOVE POLLEN ARE CALLED POLLINATORS.

SPREADING SEEDS

Once seeds form, they often need to move to a new space so they can grow. Seeds travel in multiple ways. Some, such as dandelion seeds, fly away in the wind.

ANIMALS HELP SPREAD SOME SEEDS, TOO. THEY EAT PLANTS, THEN POOP THE SEEDS OUT IN A NEW PLACE.

WILD WEEDS

Depending on where a flower grows, it might be called a different thing. Weeds are plants that grow where people don't want them to be. In nature, these same flowers are called wildflowers.

DAISIES CAN BE WILDFLOWERS OR WEEDS.

BULBS AND SEEDS

Once a seed is in a new place, it needs plenty of water and nutrients. Soon, it will grow into a new plant and make seeds of its own.

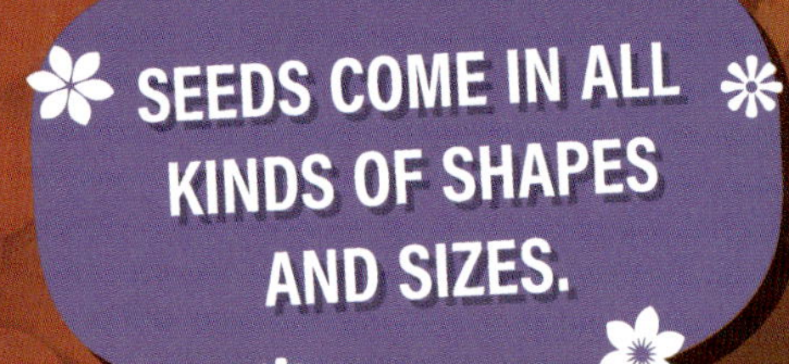

Some plants grow from bulbs. A bulb stores the plant's **energy** and nutrients below the soil during the colder months. Then, the plant regrows when the weather changes.

TULIPS GROW FROM BULBS.

FLOWER NEEDS

Plants make their own food with the things around them. The roots take in water and nutrients from the soil. The leaves collect sunlight and **carbon dioxide**. Then, plants use these things to make food.

Some plants look different at different times of the day. Lotus flowers open during the day and close at night. These plants are open when their pollinators are most active.

A LOTUS AT NIGHT

A LOTUS DURING THE DAY

HELPING HUMANS

People use flowers in lots of different ways. Many flowers are bright and colorful, so they are often used for **decoration** or given as gifts.

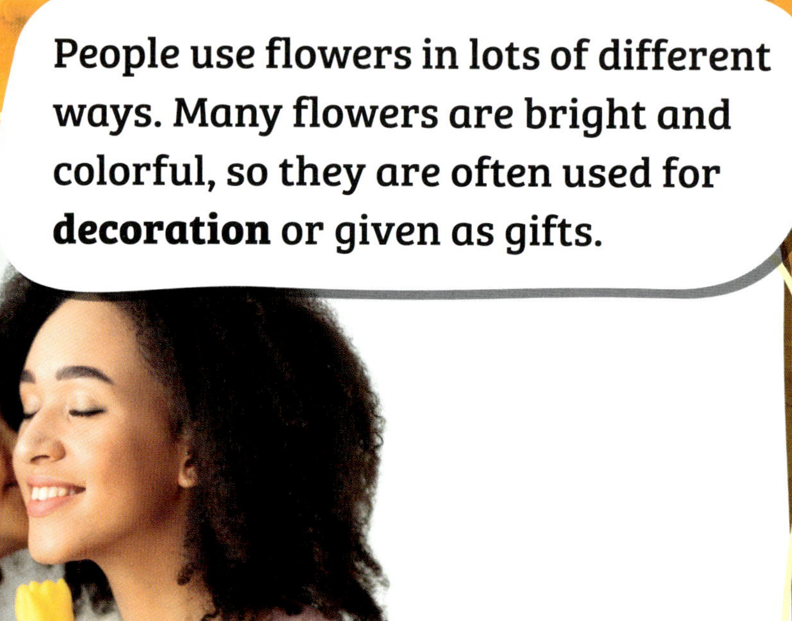

SOME PLANTS CAN MAKE YOU SICK. ALWAYS ASK A GROWN-UP BEFORE PICKING PLANTS.

Lavender and rose flowers have strong smells. They are often used to make perfumes. Some flowers, such as vanilla, are used in foods. Vanilla is common in baked goods.

VANILLA ICE CREAM USES **SEEDPODS** FROM THESE FLOWERS.

IDENTIFYING FLOWERS

Flowers grow on many types of plants. Can you match the descriptions below to the pictures on page 21?

1. Cacti often grow in hot places. Many have sharp spikes as well as colorful flowers.

2. Daisies are small wildflowers or weeds. They often have white petals and yellow middles.

3. Before apple trees grow fruit, they have small flowers. The flowers are often pink or white.

Answers: 1) Cacti are B.
2) Daisies are C. 3) Apple tree flowers are A.

FINDING FLOWERS

Flowering plants grow all over the world. Are there wildflowers or flowering weeds growing in your favorite park?

Next time you go outside, look at the plants near you. Do any of them have flowers? What colors are they? Write down what you see. There are plenty of plants to explore!

GLOSSARY

attract to cause interest

blossom to grow and open

carbon dioxide a gas that plants need to survive

decoration something that makes a thing or place look nicer

energy the power needed by all living things to grow and stay alive

insects small animals that have six legs and three main body parts

nutrients natural substances that plants and animals need to grow and stay healthy

reproduce to make more of a living thing

seedpods protective cases that hold the seeds of some plants

INDEX